MCR'

Essential Science

Earth,
Moon
& Sun

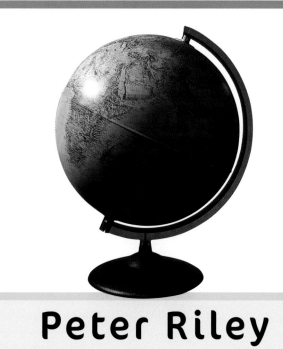

Peter Riley

A⁺
Smart Apple Media

This book has been published in cooperation with Franklin Watts.

Editor: Rachel Tonkin, Designer: Proof Books, Picture researcher: Diana Morris, Illustrations: Ian Thompson

Picture credits:
Macduff Everton/Corbis: 11; Nick Gundeson/Corbis: 17; Imagestate/Alamy: cover l; Frank Krahmer/zefa/Corbis: 18; Werner A. Miller/Corbis: 25; NASA: cover br, 3t, 6, 7l, 7r, 8t, 8b, 13, 26, 27, 28cl; Picturepoint/Topham: cover tr; Roger Ressmeyer/Corbis: 4bl; Guenter Rossenbach/Corbis: 4tr; Robin Scagell/SPL: 9; Raoul Slater/WWI/Still Pictures: cover cr; Tom Walker/Getty Images: 21; Ron Watts/Corbis: 12, 28br.

All other images: Andy Crawford

With thanks to our model: Liam Cheung

Published in the United States by Smart Apple Media
2140 Howard Drive West, North Mankato, Minnesota 56003

Library of Congress Cataloging-in-Publication Data

Riley, Peter D.
Earth, moon & sun / by Peter Riley.
p. cm. — (Essential science)
Includes index.
ISBN-13: 978-1-59920-025-5
1. Earth—Juvenile literature. 2. Solar system—Juvenile literature. 3. Moon—Juvenile literature. I. Title. II. Title: Earth, moon, and sun.

QB631.4.R564 2007
525—dc22   2006030987

9 8 7 6 5 4 3 2 1

CONTENTS

EARTH, MOON, AND SUN

Today, most people know that Earth, the moon, and the sun are almost spherical (shaped like a ball). In the past, however, people had other ideas.

As ships go over the horizon, their hulls disappear first.

Flat Earth

People used to think that Earth was flat. They thought that you just went across its surface until you came to the edge. However, if you watch a ship sailing away, it does not get smaller and smaller as it would if Earth was flat. It disappears in a certain order. The hull disappears, then the cabins above the hull, then the funnels, and finally the masts. This suggests that Earth is curved.

You can see the constellation called Orion, which has three stars in a row.

The stars provide a clue

Ancient people grouped stars together into constellations so that they could recognize different parts of the sky. If Earth was flat, the same constellations should appear in the sky wherever they went. When people traveled far to the north or south, they found that some constellations disappeared over the horizon and new ones appeared over the opposite horizon. This also suggested that Earth is curved and could be spherical.

Final proof

When spacecraft, such as satellites, were launched more than 40 years ago, they carried cameras and sent back pictures of Earth. The pictures showed that Earth was almost spherical.

The sun and the moon

The sun appears as a circular shape all the time, which suggests that it is spherical. You must never look directly at the sun because it is so bright that it can blind you. The moon sometimes appears circular, which suggests that it is also spherical. The other shapes of the moon, called phases, are due to the way sunlight shines on it.

The shape of the moon we see is made by the sun shining on it, like this flashlight on a ball.

Data

When scientists do experiments, they make observations, take measurements, and record the findings. This information is called data. It may be recorded in the form of a table, bar graph, or line graph. Collect some data about the moon by trying this activity.

Date	1st	2nd	3rd	4th	5th
Moon shape	🌙				

Prepare a table like the one shown here. Try to look at the moon each night and draw its shape in the boxes. How does your data compare?

You will find data on many pages in this book. Can you answer all of the questions?

THE SOLAR SYSTEM

Where are Earth, the moon, and the sun in space? What is a galaxy? What is the difference between a planet and a moon?

What is the solar system?

The solar system is made up of the sun, the planets, and other bodies that orbit the sun, including moons, asteroids, and comets. The sun is a star. Other stars also have planets and moons orbiting them.

The planets

There are eight planets in the solar system. They are divided into four small, rocky planets and four large planets that are mostly composed of gas and are called gas giants. The rocky planets are Mercury, Venus, Earth, and Mars. The gas giants are Jupiter, Saturn, Uranus, and Neptune.

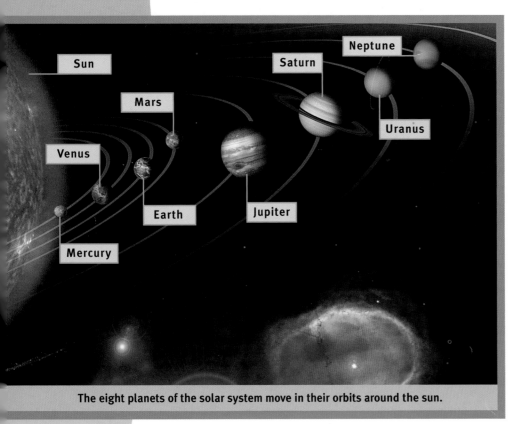

Sun

Neptune

Saturn

Mars

Venus

Uranus

Earth

Jupiter

Mercury

The eight planets of the solar system move in their orbits around the sun.

Orbits

An orbit is the path a planet travels around a star. It is also the path of a moon around a planet. The word orbit can be used to describe the movement of a planet. For example, Earth orbits the sun once a year.

Planets and moons

A large space object that moves around a star is called a planet. A smaller space object that moves around a planet is called a moon. There may be many planets moving around a star and many moons moving around a planet.

Comets

A comet is a lump of rock and ice. It has an orbit that takes it close to the sun and then far away beyond Neptune. As a comet moves close to the sun, some of the ice melts and forms a long, cloudy tail.

A comet's tail points away from the sun.

Galaxies

If you could travel through the universe, you would see huge groups of millions of stars. They are called galaxies. Some galaxies are like clouds and do not have a special shape. Other galaxies are elliptical or spiral in shape. The sun is a star in a spiral galaxy called the Milky Way.

The solar system is in a spiral galaxy called the Milky Way.

Asteroids

A huge number of rocks form a ring between the orbits of Mars and Jupiter. The rocks are called asteroids, and the ring is called the asteroid belt.

Planet distance

1 Is the orbit of Mars closer to Earth's orbit than the orbit of Venus?

2 How much faster than Mars does Mercury travel?

3 How does the speed of planets change as they get farther away from the sun?

Planet	Distance to sun millions of miles (km)	Speed in orbit miles per second (km/s)
Mercury	36 (58)	30 (48)
Venus	67 (108)	22 (35)
Earth	93 (150)	19 (30)
Mars	142 (228)	15 (24)

THE STARS AND THE SUN

The sun is a star, but where do stars come from? How do they form?

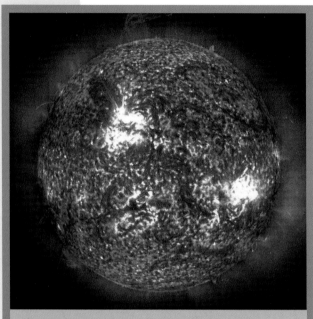

The sun gives out huge amounts of light and heat. Note the solar flare near the top (see opposite).

The big bang

Scientists believe an explosion called the big bang created the universe about 13 billion years ago. It created new substances—two gases called hydrogen and helium. Stars most likely began as clouds of hydrogen and dust. The force of gravity pulled the clouds together to form thicker and thicker clumps. These clumps formed young stars, which then began to heat up. Once a star reaches a certain temperature, the hydrogen in it begins to burn and release light. This lasts for billions of years until the hydrogen is used up.

Old stars to new

When a star has only a small amount of hydrogen remaining, it may fade away and release large amounts of dust, or it may explode and form a supernova. The gases and dust that are released spread out through space and make clouds in which more stars form. The sun formed in a gas cloud five billion years ago.

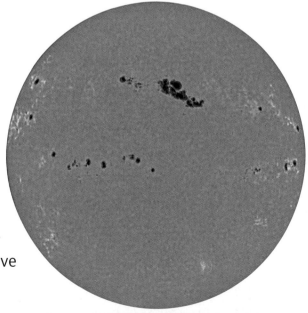

The sun has spots on its surface (see opposite).

Spots and flares

It is 7,230 °F (4,000 °C) on most of the sun's surface, but inside, many cooler substances are churning. They make parts of the sun act like a magnet. The pull of magnetic forces makes dark patches of cooler gas on the surface called sunspots. The churning of substances also shoots out huge clouds of gas called solar flares.

The spinning sun

If the sun is viewed every day through a telescope as shown in the picture, the sunspots move. They show that the sun is slowly turning. It takes 30 days for the sun to turn around once.

The sun can be studied by focusing a picture of it on a screen using a special type of telescope.

How near are the stars?

The distance of stars from Earth is measured in light years. A light year is the distance traveled by a ray of light in one year—six trillion miles (9.5 trillion km). Here are the distances of some stars from Earth.

1 Which one is the closest?

2 Which one is the farthest?

3 Think of the light reaching Earth from Polaris tonight. In which year did it leave the star?

4 In which year were you born? When did light reaching Earth in that year from Betelgeuse begin its journey?

Star	Distance in light-years
Polaris	6
Deneb	1,006
Regulus	84
Arcturus	36
Betelgeuse	520

EARTH AND GRAVITY

Earth is a huge ball of rock in space. The pull of gravity moves Earth around the sun and the moon around Earth.

How Earth formed

Earth and the other planets formed from a spinning disc of gas and dust around the sun. The spinning of the disc gave the planets their spins and the energy to move through space.

Gravity between the sun and Earth

A force of gravity exists between any two objects in the universe. The sun's force of gravity pulls on Earth as it tries to move in a straight line through space. The force of the sun pulls Earth toward it so that Earth follows an elliptical path called an orbit around the sun. The sun's gravity pulls on the other planets in the solar system and makes them travel in orbits around the sun, too. The planets' forces of gravity pull on the sun and make it wobble slightly as it spins.

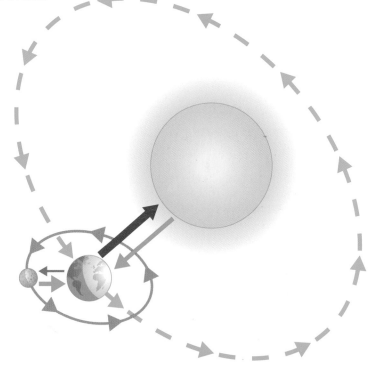

The forces between Earth, the moon, and the sun.

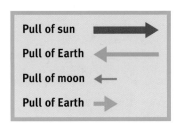

Pull of sun	➡
Pull of Earth	⬅
Pull of moon	←
Pull of Earth	→

Gravity between Earth and the moon

As the moon tries to move out into space, the pull from Earth's gravity is just strong enough to keep pulling the moon back toward Earth. This makes the moon travel around Earth in an orbit. The moon's gravity is weaker than Earth's, but its pull on Earth is strong enough to make the surface of Earth's oceans and seas rise and fall.

The moon's gravity makes tides rise and fall on the shore.

Changing weight

Weight is due to the pull of Earth's gravity on the mass of an object. The table shows how the weight of a mass changes as it moves away from Earth.

1 By how much has the weight changed as it has gone into space?
2 Does the pull of gravity get stronger, weaker, or stay the same as an object moves away from Earth?
3 What do you think would happen to the object's weight as it moved farther from Earth?

Mass (kg)	Weight (pounds) on Earth's surface	Weight (pounds) per 9,320 miles (15,000 km) in space
1	2.2	0.4

THE MOON

The moon is our nearest neighbor in space. It may have formed from a huge crash between planets. If you could visit the moon, you would find that it is a silent world of rocks and dust.

The big crash

Nobody is sure how the moon formed, but many scientists believe that about four and a half billion years ago, Earth was struck by a planet roughly the size of Mars. The crash produced great heat, which melted the planet and turned some of it into vapor that rushed out into space. The vapor cooled as it moved away and formed a ring of rocky lumps around Earth. In time, these lumps of rock crashed together to form the moon.

The moon does not just appear in the night sky but also appears in the daytime sky.

If you were to visit the moon, you would find that much of it is covered in dust. The footprints you left behind would last for millions of years because there is no atmosphere to blow the dust around. Unlike Earth, which has air, the moon has no gases to carry sound. You would find that the moon is a silent place.

Astronauts collected rock samples from the moon that have helped scientists understand how the moon may have formed.

On the moon's surface

If you look at a full moon, you can see that part of its surface is white and part of it is gray. The white parts are formed by mountains, and the gray parts are formed by plains covered in lava that cooled and hardened a long time ago. When you look at the moon with binoculars or a small telescope, you can see circles on the surface. These are craters made by asteroids that crashed into the moon's surface millions of years ago.

Planets and their moons

Here are the planets in the solar system that have moons.

1 Two planets do not have any moons. Look at the picture of the solar system on page 6 and this table. Which ones are they?
2 How does the number of moons around each planet change as you move outward from Earth to Neptune?

Planet	number of moons
Earth	1
Mars	2
Jupiter	28
Saturn	30
Uranus	21
Neptune	8

SUN, MOON, AND EARTH

The sun, the moon, and Earth are the three objects in space that everyone knows. How big are they, what are the distances between them, and why do the moon and sun seem the same size?

How big are they?

The sun has a diameter of 864,948 miles (1,392,000 km). The moon has a diameter of 2,160 miles (3,476 km). Earth has a diameter of 7,926 miles (12,756 km).

If you think of the sun as the size of a beach ball, Earth the size of a pea, and the moon the size of a tiny bead, you can get some idea of how their sizes compare.

How far away is the moon?

The moon is 238,917 miles (384,500 km) from Earth.

How far away is the sun?

The sun is about 92,957,130 miles (149,600,000 km) from Earth.

The effect of distance

The sun and the moon appear to be about the same size in the sky. This is because the moon is very close to Earth and the sun is a long way away. The short distance of the small moon from Earth makes it appear large. The long distance of the huge sun from Earth makes it appear small.

When the beach ball is moved into the distance, it appears smaller than it really is.

An eclipse of the sun

As the moon travels in its orbit around Earth, it sometimes passes directly between the sun and Earth. When this happens, an eclipse of the sun occurs, and the light of the sun is blocked by the moon moving in front of it.

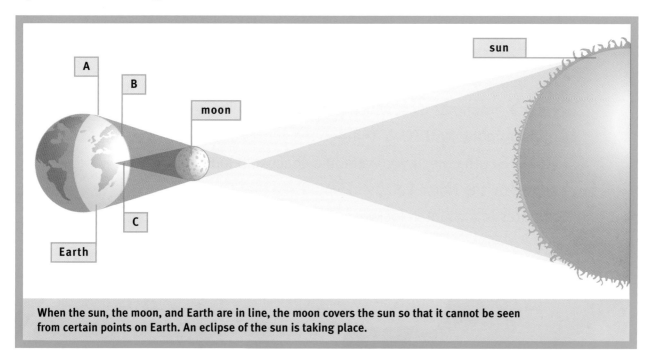

When the sun, the moon, and Earth are in line, the moon covers the sun so that it cannot be seen from certain points on Earth. An eclipse of the sun is taking place.

An eclipse of the moon

Sometimes Earth passes directly between the sun and the moon and stops the sun's light from reaching the moon. When this happens, an eclipse of the moon occurs, and a shadow of Earth is cast on its surface. The light from the sun is blocked by Earth.

Where on Earth does an eclipse of the sun occur?

A total eclipse does not occur on all parts of Earth—just where the moon's shadow, the umbra, is darkest. In the paler shadow, called the penumbra, a partial eclipse is seen.

Look at the diagram above and see if you can figure out the answers to the questions.

1 Where will a total eclipse occur, at point A, B, or C?

2 Where will a partial eclipse occur?

3 In which place will an eclipse not occur?

SPINNING EARTH

Earth spins around in space, and this gives us day and night.

Rotation

The spinning movement is also called rotation. Earth rotates around its axis, which is an imaginary line that runs from the North Pole through the center of Earth to the South Pole. If you were in a spaceship looking down on the North Pole, you would see that Earth rotates in a counterclockwise direction.

day

night

Where the light shines on Earth, it is daytime. Where the light does not shine, it is nighttime.

Daytime and nighttime

It takes Earth 24 hours to make one rotation. We call this time period a day. As Earth rotates, each part spends some time facing toward the sun (daytime) and some time facing away from it (nighttime).

The tilting Earth

The axis of Earth is tilted at 23.5 degrees from a vertical line running through Earth's center. Earth always tilts in the same direction as it moves around the sun (see page 22).

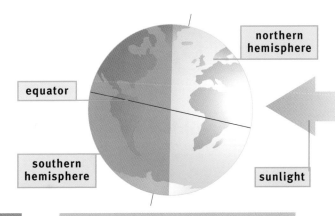

northern hemisphere

equator

southern hemisphere

sunlight

The tilt of Earth means that some parts of Earth are tipped toward the light and some parts are tipped away from it.

This city is in a hemisphere tilted away from the sun, so it starts to get dark early.

Hemispheres

There is an imaginary line around Earth called the equator. The region above it is called the northern hemisphere, and the region below it is called the southern hemisphere. When a hemisphere is tilted toward the sun, the places in it receive more than 12 hours of daylight. When it is tilted away from the sun, the places receive fewer than 12 hours of daylight.

Times to spin

All planets spin. Here are the times it takes some of the planets to spin around once:

1 Which planets have longer days than Earth?
2 Look at the picture of the planets on page 6. Which planets have the shorter days—small planets or large planets?

Planet	Time length of spin
Mercury	1,408 hrs, 48 mins
Venus	5,832 hrs
Mars	24 hrs, 37 mins
Jupiter	9 hrs, 55 mins
Saturn	10 hrs, 39 mins
Uranus	17 hrs, 14 mins
Neptune	16 hrs, 7 mins

THE PATH OF THE SUN

The sun appears to follow a path across the sky.

The sun rises over the eastern horizon at dawn and disappears over the western horizon at sunset.

The horizon

The horizon is the place where the sky appears to meet the ground. If you are at the coast, the horizon is where the sky seems to meet the surface of the ocean. If you are inland, it can be the place where the sky meets hilltops, trees, or the roofs of buildings. During the day, the sun appears to move across the sky. This is not caused by the sun moving but by Earth turning on its axis.

Using shadows

We cannot look directly at the sun because it can blind us. But we can use a yardstick and look at the shadows it casts in the sunlight. A shadow is made when light strikes an opaque object. When a shadow forms, it points in the opposite direction of the sun. If a compass is used with the yardstick, the direction in which the shadow points can be used to find the direction of the sun. For example, if the shadow points west, then the sun is in the east.

The length of the shadow can be used to find the height of the sun in the sky. For example, when the shadow is long, the sun is low in the sky, and when the shadow is short, the sun is high in the sky.

A yardstick can be used to find how the position of the sun changes during the day.

The sun follows a curved path across the sky.

Where is the sun?

The table shows the direction and length of shadows cast by a yardstick.

Time	Shadow direction	Shadow length inches (cm)
6:00 A.M.	west	39 (100)
9:00 A.M.	northwest	29.5 (75)
Noon	north	20 (50)
3:00 P.M.	northeast	29.5 (75)
6:00 P.M.	east	39 (100)

1 In which part of the sky is the sun at each of the five times shown in the table?

2 How does the shadow length change during the day?

3 When is the sun highest in the sky?

4 When is the sun lowest in the sky?

THE SUN'S CHANGING PATH

The height and length of the sun's path across the sky changes during the year.

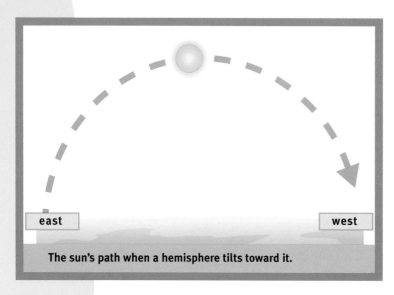

The sun's path when a hemisphere tilts toward it.

High in the sky

When a hemisphere (see page 17) is tilted toward the sun, sunrise occurs farther to the east along the horizon. The sun rises high in the sky and sets farther to the west. It spends a long time in the sky, and the days are long.

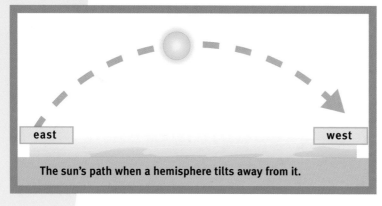

The sun's path when a hemisphere tilts away from it.

Low in the sky

When a hemisphere is tilted away from the sun, sunrise occurs farther to the west. The sun does not rise as high in the sky and sets farther toward the east. It spends a much shorter time in the sky, and the days are short.

Long and short days

The tilt of Earth is the main cause of the different seasons (see page 22). It also means that the length of days and nights varies at different times of the year, depending on where a place is in relation to the equator. Days get longer or shorter according to the season and the proximity to the poles.

The midnight sun

When the North Pole or the South Pole is tilted toward the sun, the places nearby receive sunlight for 24 hours each day, even at midnight. The sun does not set, it just dips low toward the horizon then rises again.

The darkest days

When the North Pole or the South Pole is tilted away from the sun, the places nearby do not receive any sunlight. The sun does not rise in the sky, so places have 24 hours of darkness each day.

This picture was taken with a camera that can take an image for 24 hours. It shows the path the sun takes at a pole when the pole is tilted toward the sun.

How times change

Here are the times for sunrise and sunset at a place in the northern hemisphere. The times were recorded on one day of each month.

1 Make a graph of the data. Put the time on the horizontal x axis from 1:00 A.M. to midnight and the months on the vertical y axis.

2 How do the sunrise and sunset times change?

3 How does the day length change each month?

4 What do you predict will happen to the day length the rest of the year?

Month	Sunrise	Sunset
January	8:00 A.M.	4:30 P.M.
February	7:30 A.M.	5:00 P.M.
March	6:00 A.M.	6:00 P.M.
April	5:30 A.M.	7:30 P.M.
May	5:00 A.M.	8:30 P.M.
June	4:30 A.M.	10:00 P.M.
July	5:00 A.M.	8:30 P.M.

A YEAR ON EARTH

**It takes a year for Earth to travel around the sun.
In many places, the year is divided into four seasons.**

Years and leap years

Earth takes 365.25 rotations, or days, to travel around the sun. This period of time is called a year. Because the number of days is not exact, people have made most years into 365 days. But every fourth year has 366 days and is called a leap year.

The seasons

Winter

When a hemisphere is tilted away from the sun, it is winter. The sun does not spend a long time in the sky (see page 20), so it gives little heat to Earth's surface, and the weather is cold. There is one day that has a shorter period of daylight than any other day. This day is called the winter solstice.

Spring

In the spring, the hemisphere is neither tilting toward nor away from the sun. The path of the sun has become longer than in the winter, and more heat reaches Earth's surface. There is one day that has the same number of hours of daylight and darkness. This day is called the spring equinox.

Summer

When a hemisphere is tilted toward the sun, it is summer. The sun spends a long time in the sky and gives a great deal of heat to Earth's surface, which makes the weather hot. There is one day that has a longer period of daylight than any other day of the year. This day is called the summer solstice.

Fall

In the fall, the hemisphere is neither tilting toward nor away from the sun. The path of the sun has become shorter than in the summer, and less heat reaches Earth's surface. There is one day that has the same number of hours of daylight and darkness. This day is called the fall equinox.

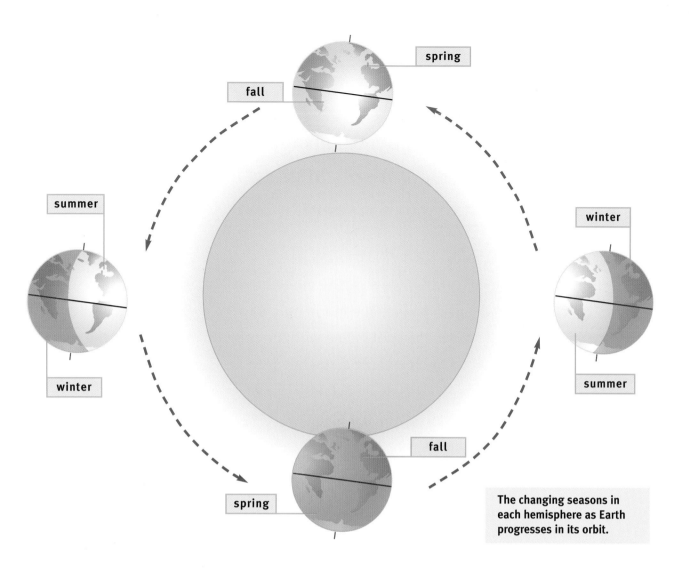

The changing seasons in each hemisphere as Earth progresses in its orbit.

Opposite seasons

While the northern hemisphere has winter, spring, summer, and fall, the southern hemisphere has the opposite—summer, fall, winter, and spring. This is because the southern hemisphere tilts in the opposite direction of the northern hemisphere.

How far does Earth travel?

Earth travels in its orbit at a speed of about 6,462 miles (10,400 km) per hour.

1 How far does it travel in 10 hours?

2 How far does it travel in 24 hours?

3 How far does it travel in 1 minute?

THE MOON IN ITS ORBIT

The moon moves in a path around Earth. As it travels, different amounts of its surface are lit by the sun and make it seem to change shape.

The moon's orbit

As Earth moves around the sun, the moon moves in a counterclockwise orbit around Earth. It takes the moon 29.5 days to travel around Earth. The orbit of the moon is not in line with the orbit of Earth around the sun. If it was, the moon would come between the sun and Earth at each new moon and cause an eclipse. The moon spins as it moves in its orbit. The speed at which it spins keeps the same side of the moon always facing Earth.

The phases of the moon

The moon does not produce light like the sun does. It shines by the sunlight that is reflected from its surface. The area of the moon that we can see from Earth that reflects light changes as the moon moves in its orbit. These different areas are known as phases. They occur in order each month as the diagram shows.

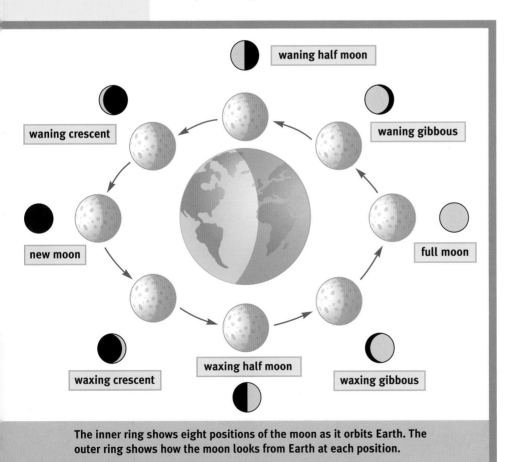

waning half moon

waning crescent

waning gibbous

new moon

full moon

waxing crescent

waxing half moon

waxing gibbous

The inner ring shows eight positions of the moon as it orbits Earth. The outer ring shows how the moon looks from Earth at each position.

The moon forms a crescent when it is waxing and waning.

The new moon

At each new moon, the moon is a little above or below the sun in the sky, so an eclipse of the sun does not occur.

At this time, the surface of the moon facing Earth is in complete darkness and cannot be seen. After a day, a crescent of light can be seen on the moon's surface. This crescent phase is what most people call the new moon.

Waxing and waning

The moon is said to be waxing when the size of its shining surface increases each night. The moon is said to be waning when the size of its shining surface decreases each night.

Phases

1 What are the three phases of the moon shown here?
2 In what order do they occur after a new moon as the moon travels in its orbit?

A

B

C

EXPLORING SPACE

People who lived long ago made many discoveries about space simply by looking at the sky and noticing changes over time. Today, we have many kinds of equipment to help us find out more.

Rocket engines fire to lift this spacecraft into the sky.

Early discoveries

People's early discoveries of space were based on observation with the naked eye. They could see and record the path of the sun, the phases of the moon, and the position of the stars, which did not move, and the planets, which did move. The word "planet" means "wanderer." They explained these things in various ways (see panel) but some people began to question these ideas. In particular, the invention of the telescope allowed astronomers to study the skies in even more detail. Slowly, people's ideas about space began to change.

The rocket engine

More powerful telescopes were developed, but it was the invention of the rocket engine that led to the development of spacecraft. The rocket engine is powerful enough to push a spacecraft away from the pull of Earth's gravity.

Humans in space

Some spacecraft carry humans. These spacecraft, such as the space shuttle, may take astronauts to and from space. There are also space stations in which humans live that orbit Earth. The people living in space stations study the effects of living in space. The results of their investigations will help design spacecraft to visit other planets, such as Mars.

Space probes

Probes carry instruments to measure the conditions in space and cameras to take photographs. Some probes that land on other planets or moons carry vehicles that can travel over their surfaces to examine rocks and measure the conditions in the environment.

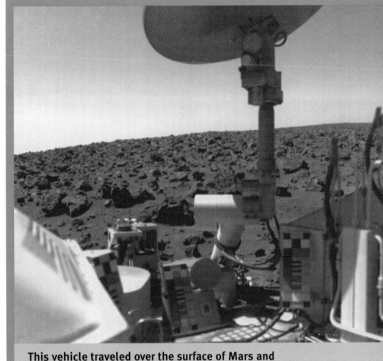

This vehicle traveled over the surface of Mars and carried equipment to investigate the conditions there.

Early discoveries

For a long time, people believed that Earth was the center of the universe and everything moved around it. They also believed that comets were clouds in the air.

Tycho Brahe (1546–1601) studied a comet with the naked eye. He found that it was farther away than the moon was and appeared to move through space.

Galileo (1564–1642) built a telescope to see farther into space. He discovered moons moving around Jupiter.

Johannes Kepler (1571–1630) studied how planets, including Earth, moved and found that they moved in elliptical orbits around the sun.

1 What early beliefs did Tycho Brahe prove to be wrong?

2 Why were people surprised by Galileo's observations of the moons?

3 Why do you think people did not like Kepler's discovery?

CAN YOU REMEMBER THE ESSENTIALS?

Here are the essential science facts about Earth, the moon, and the sun. They are presented in the order you read about them in the book. Spend a couple of minutes learning each set of facts. If you can learn them all, you know all of the essentials about Earth, the moon, and the sun.

The solar system (pages 6-7)

The solar system is made up of the sun and the eight planets that revolve around it.
A planet moves around the sun. A moon moves around a planet. An orbit is a path taken by a planet or moon in space.

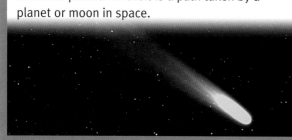

Earth and gravity
(pages 10-11)

Earth formed from a disc of gas and dust. The sun's gravity pulls Earth around in its orbit. Earth's gravity pulls the moon around it in an orbit.

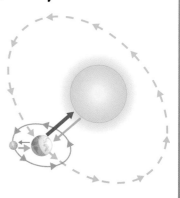

The stars and the sun
(pages 8-9)

It is believed that the universe began with an explosion called the big bang.
The sun is made from two gases—hydrogen and helium.
There are spots and flares on the surface of the sun.
The sun rotates once every 30 days.

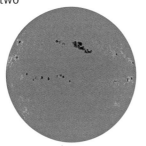

The moon (pages 12-13)

The moon may have formed when two planets crashed together.
The white parts of the moon are mountains.
The gray parts of the moon are plains.
The circles you can see on the moon are called craters.
The moon does not have an atmosphere.

Sun, moon, and Earth
(pages 14–15)

The sun is much larger than
Earth and the moon.
The sun is much farther away
from Earth than the moon is.
The great distance between the
sun and moon makes the sun appear to be
the same size as the moon.
An eclipse of the sun occurs when the moon
passes between the sun and Earth.

A year on Earth (pages 22–23)

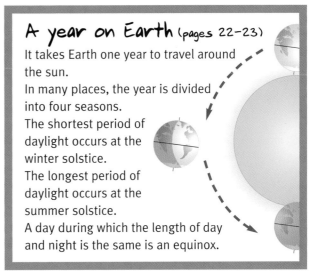

It takes Earth one year to travel around
the sun.
In many places, the year is divided
into four seasons.
The shortest period of
daylight occurs at the
winter solstice.
The longest period of
daylight occurs at the
summer solstice.
A day during which the length of day
and night is the same is an equinox.

Spinning Earth (pages 16–17)

Earth rotates around its axis.
It takes Earth a day to make one
rotation. The axis of Earth is
tilted. The tilt affects the length
of day and night at a place on
Earth's surface.

The moon in its orbit
(pages 24–25)

The moon moves in an orbit around Earth.
It takes the moon almost a month to complete
one orbit.
The moon rotates but always keeps the same
side facing Earth.
The area of light from the sun reflected from
the moon is called
a phase.
The phases of
the moon
change
as it
moves
around its
orbit.

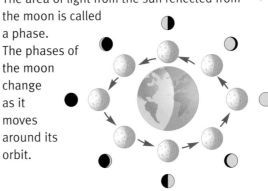

The path of the sun
(pages 18–19)

The sun appears over the eastern horizon
at dawn.
The sun rises in the sky in the morning.
The sun sinks in the sky in the
afternoon.
The sun disappears
over the western horizon at sunset.
The length and position of shadows can be used
to find the movement of the sun in the sky.

Exploring space (pages 26–27)

Early people made observations on space simply
by looking at the sky.
The telescope allows more objects in space
to be seen.
Rocket engines are used to launch spacecraft.
Space probes carry equipment to investigate
space and the objects in it.
Humans can investigate space from space
stations that are in orbit around Earth.

The sun's changing path
(pages 20–21)

When a hemisphere is tilted toward the
sun, the sun makes a long, high path in the sky.
When a hemisphere is tilted away from the
sun, the sun makes a short, low path in the sky.
When a pole is tilted toward the sun, the
sun does not set in the sky.
When a pole is tilted away from the sun,
the sun does not rise in the sky.

GLOSSARY

Asteroid A small planet.

Astronaut A person who is specially trained to live and work in space.

Atmosphere The mixture of gases that surrounds a planet or moon.

Axis An imaginary line running through the center of Earth from the North Pole to the South Pole.

Comet A large lump of rock and ice in orbit around the sun.

Constellation A group of stars named by ancient peoples to map out the night skies.

Elliptical A line that is oval in shape.

Energy Something that allows an object or a living thing to take part in an activity, such as moving or giving out light.

Equinox A time of year when day and night are the same length of time.

Galaxy A huge group of stars in space.

Gravity A force of attraction that exists between any two objects in the universe but only causes movement when one object is very much larger than the other.

Hemisphere Either the northern or southern half of Earth.

Moon The large object in orbit around Earth. It can also refer to any object in orbit around a planet.

North Pole and South Pole The points on Earth's surface at each end of Earth's axis.

Opaque Something that you cannot see through.

Orbit The path taken by a planet around a star or a moon around a planet.

Planet A large object that is in orbit around a star.

Probe An unmanned space vehicle carrying scientific instruments that is sent from Earth to explore space.

Rocket engine An engine that shoots out a jet of hot gases to produce a force to move a spacecraft.

Rotation The movement of an object around its center, such as the movement of Earth around its axis.

Solar flare Clouds of gas that shoot out from the sun.

Solstice The time when the sun either rises to its highest point in the sky or sinks to its lowest point in the sky.

Space station A space vehicle in which astronauts can live and work.

Star A huge ball of gas made from hydrogen and helium.

Sunspot A patch of cool gas on the sun's surface.

Supernova A huge star that suddenly increases in brightness and releases a huge amount of energy. This happens because the inside of the star collapses and triggers a violent explosion.

Universe All of space and everything that is in it.

Weight The force of an object pressing down toward the center of Earth as a result of gravity.

ANSWERS

The solar system (pages 6–7)

1 No.
2 Twice as fast, or 15 miles (24 km) per second faster.
3 It decreases.

The stars and the sun (pages 8–9)

1 Polaris.
2 Deneb.
3 Six years before the date you saw the star.
4 520 years before the year you were born.

Earth and gravity (pages 10–11)

1 It has decreased by 1.8 pounds.
2 Gets weaker.
3 It would get smaller.

The moon (pages 12–13)

1 Mercury and Venus.
2 It increases to a maximum at Saturn and then decreases again.

Sun, moon, and Earth (pages 14–15)

1 C
2 B
3 A

Spinning Earth (pages 16–17)

1 Mercury, Venus, and Mars.
2 Large planets.

The path of the sun (pages 18–19)

1 6:00 A.M.—low in the east; 9:00 A.M.—higher in the southeast; noon—high in the south; 3:00 P.M. lower in the southwest; 6:00 P.M.—low in the west.
2 It decreases in the morning and increases in the afternoon.
3 At noon.
4 At 6:00 A.M. and 6:00 P.M.

The sun's changing path (pages 20–21)

2 Sunrise times get earlier until June, then get later again. Sunset times get later until June, then get earlier again.
3 It increases from January to June, then decreases from June to July.
4 It will decrease.

A year on Earth (pages 22–23)

1 64,620 miles (104,000 km).
2 155,088 miles (249,600 km).
3 107.7 miles (173.3 km).

The moon in its orbit (pages 24–25)

1 A = waning crescent; B = waxing half moon; C = waning gibbous.
2 B, C, A.

Exploring space (pages 26–27)

1 Comets were not clouds but were out in space.
2 They thought everything moved around Earth.
3 It meant that Earth was no longer the center of the universe. It was less important.

INDEX